GANESHA

ONE DAY, PARVATI, SHIVA'S WIFE, POSTED NANDI, HIS GANA,* AT THE DOOR TO HER PALACE.

I AM GOING TO HAVE MY BATH. DO NOT LET ANYONE ENTER AND DISTURB ME.

A LITTLE LATER, SHIVA CAME THERE. NANDI WAS IN A DILEMMA.

WHAT SHOULD I DO? HOW CAN I STOP HIM FROM ENTERING HIS OWN HOME?

* ATTENDANT.

ONE OF THEM HAD AN IDEA.

WHY DON'T YOU CREATE A GANA WHO WILL OWE FIRST ALLEGIANCE TO YOU?

A GOOD SUGGESTION. I SHALL.

SHE GATHERED THE SAFFRON PASTE FROM HER OWN BODY AND CREATED A BOY.

WHEN SHE FINISHED, SHE GAZED IN ADMIRATION AT HER OWN CREATION.

HOW HANDSOME HE IS! HOW STRONG HE LOOKS!

AS THEY NEARED HIM, THE YOUTH SUDDENLY JUMPED FORWARD AND—

THAT SHOULD TEACH YOU A LESSON.

BRAHMA WAS TAKEN UNAWARES.

I HAVE NOT COME TO FIGHT. I HAVE COME TO MAKE PEACE. LISTEN TO ME!

FOR AN ANSWER, THE YOUTH LIFTED HIS CLUB MENACINGLY.

DURGA TOOK THE FORM OF LIGHTNING...

...AND DESTROYED THE ENEMIES' WEAPONS BEFORE THEY COULD REACH THE BOY.

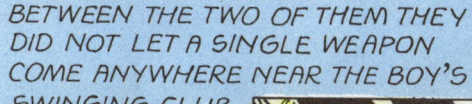

BETWEEN THE TWO OF THEM THEY DID NOT LET A SINGLE WEAPON COME ANYWHERE NEAR THE BOY'S SWINGING CLUB.

THEN THE DEVAS AND THE GANAS BECAME JUBILANT.

BUT SHIVA WAS TROUBLED.

ALAS! WHAT HAVE I DONE? HOW SHALL I FACE PARVATI? HE WAS CREATED BY HER. THAT MADE HIM MY SON TOO.

MEANWHILE, WHEN PARVATI LEARNT OF HER SON'S DEATH—

MY SON WAS KILLED BY UNFAIR MEANS. FOR THIS THE DEVAS AND GANAS SHALL ALL DIE.

OUT OF HER FURY, SHE CREATED HUNDREDS AND THOUSANDS OF SHAKTIS.

O MOTHER, WHAT IS YOUR COMMAND?

DESTROY ALL THE DEVAS AND GANAS. DEVOUR THEM.

THE SHAKTIS IMMEDIATELY SET ABOUT CARRYING OUT HER COMMAND. BRAHMA AND VISHNU WERE TERRIFIED.

PARVATI MUST BE APPEASED.

IT WAS A SINGLE-TUSKED ELEPHANT THAT MET THEM.

THEY BROUGHT THE HEAD BACK AND FITTED IT TO THE BODY OF THE BOY.

THE BOY SAT UP.